Life is Good

Peter Skillen

ISBN-13:
978-1497399136

ISBN-10:
1497399130

Table of Contents

Foreword

It is my privilege to be writing the foreword for this fantastic book.

I first met Peter after releasing my own book late in 2013, a book that exceeded my expectations. Peter had released 'The Twelve Step Warrior' and it had been recommended to me time and time again. When I finally read it, I felt I simply had to meet Peter to congratulate him on his journey so far.

I began to train with Peter at his kickboxing classes, something I thought I'd never get back into as confidence was at an all time low. He has taught me that I can only move forwards, and this has had a huge, positive impact on my life.

Not only is Peter an inspiration, he has changed many lives for the better and continues to do so.

I was privileged to be one of the first to read 'Life is Good' and I've been looking forward to its much anticipated release. It's much more than a book of inspirational thoughts and affirmations; it's the wisdom of Peter's experiences.

I highly recommend this book, I couldn't put it down and read it throughout the night with my eyes wide open.

Life IS good, if you can learn to embrace it.

Moll French
International Bestselling Author of
Dirty Old Man (A True Story)

Life is Good

A few years ago, I wrote a book called *The Twelve-Step Warrior*, and in that book I talk about the life I used to lead. I was a drunk. A depressed, angry, violent and uneducated drunk.

In *The Twelve-Step Warrior,* I tell the story of abuses that took place during my childhood, the separation of my family, and my descent into a world of addiction, violence and depression. I also write about how I drew on my last reserves to find a way out of the darkness I had surrounded myself with and how I eventually made something of my life.

Since writing *The Twelve-Step Warrior,* I have gone on to gain multiple black belts from some of the world's top martial artists. I have re-educated myself, gaining a degree (BSc (Hons)) in the process. I have become a scriptwriter and filmmaker, as well as gaining

3

employment as a teacher. I am now teaching some of the most inspiring young people I have ever met, all of whom have had similar childhoods to mine.

While writing *The Twelve-Step Warrior,* I spoke about my early life and how I loved the closeness of my family home. I wrote about how life was good and how I felt loved by my large, loving family. I was happy writing about and remembering the hot, sunny days I spent with my family and friends, but eventually I hit a point in my young life that was full of shame.

I tried to write it down time and time again, but fear and shame overwhelmed me. The harder I tried the harder it became, until eventually it broke me. I began to cry, and I cried so much that it hurt me. I tried to leave my keyboard and walk away, and again the spectre of fear loomed heavy in the air.

I sat with tears streaming down my face, my heart beating fast. I was so full of fear; fear of the story I was about to tell. I was about to admit defeat, but then I remembered all the days that had gone before and the feeling of defeat I had felt every other time I had written, read and deleted. It was now or never, so, tentatively and slowly, with tears running down my face, I typed the story of abuse that blighted my childhood. The more I typed the more I cried, but I couldn't stop. I seeped tears and typed pain, heartache and shame into every word I wrote.

One day, with fear on my back, listening to the thoughts of self-doubt, a revelation suddenly came to me. In order to confront my fears and finally rid myself of these past fears, I had to finish *The Twelve-Step Warrior* – warts and all – the story of my dark past.

I had to continue writing. It was hard, but it taught me many things. The main thing it taught me was that, in order for us to grow, we have to keep going no matter how hard it gets. I had to pass through the darkness to get to the light.

One of the other things I discovered was that I enjoyed writing so much that I now write on a daily basis. I find it cathartic, cleansing almost, and this book is full of these writings, short stories and musings. I have found that the more I write the more I discover about myself and about how I see the world.

When I wrote this collection of thoughts, I didn't plan what I was going to write down. I just sat down and wrote, and what came out seemed to make sense to me. It also seemed to inspire many of the people who read them, and that is why I have put them together in this book. I hope they will also inspire you.

Lego Lifestyle

The kids' toy known as Lego is a simple, plastic blob that has been moulded into the shape of a brick in a variety colours. This plastic brick provides hours and hours of entertainment for children all around the world. Each Christmas, millions of kids will open their presents to find a small box of these plastic bricks inside. Some of these kids will be disappointed that they haven't received the latest video game or a flashy mountain bike or the next big gadget. Except the dreamers, that is.

You see, although Lego may seem like a simple toy to some, it is a powerful gift of knowledge to others. This little piece of coloured plastic isn't as simple as you might think. For it to work it has to be strong enough to support many other bricks, while at the same time it must be precise enough to grip with just the right amount of pressure so that it can be released at any time. More than fifteen billion of these simple plastic bricks are made every year, but they are made with such precision that only eighteen in every million pieces are considered to be defective. Eighteen in every million! WOW! Now that is precise.

Each piece has to be able to fit the next to provide stability and structure, and if you have seen some of the structures that can be built with Lego you'll understand what I'm saying here. With just a few pieces, the youngest child can build representations of everyday structures, mainly starting with representations of mum or dad or a house or, for me as a child, a space rocket. I always was a dreamer. There are people around the world who, with time, effort, planning and commitment, are able to build grand structures with so much attention to detail that you forget you're looking at a child's toy.

In fact, there is a whole theme park dedicated to this simple building block, and it receives hundreds of thousands of visitors every year. Some travel across the world to be in this place amid millions of multi-coloured plastic building blocks. Why? What kind of a geek would travel halfway around the world or commit thousands of hours of their time to play with a child's toy?

Well, maybe these people understand something that other people don't. Maybe they have an understanding of life that many of us often miss. Maybe they have found the secret!

You see, if we were all a little more Lego-cultured, maybe, just maybe, we could change ourselves or – even better – we could change the world.Here's the thing. Let's say we all became Lego builders of life. Let's say we took a look at our own simple bricks – in this case our bodies – and tried to be a little bit more precise with them.

The Lego manufacturer manages just eighteen defects in a million. Surely that's enough to make you think they've got to be doing something right, right?If we become more mindful of what goes into our bricks (sorry, bodies), surely the defected output would be lower.

For the most part, we all start life like a piece of Lego. Some of us are standard bricks, while others are smaller or multi-coloured bricks. There are bricks of different shapes and sizes. Some bricks are fancy and detailed, while others – my favourite kind – are just simple bricks.

But they all do one thing. They're not all the same shape or colour, and they are not all made in the same place. But they are all Lego. So, with a little imagination, determination, time and effort, coupled with togetherness, we can build vast structures, amazing palaces and the tallest towers.

We can make people gaze in wonder and even travel thousands of miles across the world just to be in our company.With just a little bit of Lego lifestyle, we can become anything we desire to be. Our goals would only be as limited as our imaginations. Working together like Lego, we could right wrongs, build futures, achieve our dreams and support our fellow men and women.

Remember: With just a little bit of Lego lifestyle we could maybe change the world. You can achieve anything you want with just a little bit of Lego lifestyle.

Your Thoughts

Inch by Inch

We create our own futures and you can restart your day at any time. You only have to sit and think about what you really want in your life and then head

towards it, inch by inch. We have to understand that this life is not a rehearsal; we only get one shot. We all deserve a good and happy life, but to achieve this we have to take positive action. It is positive action that gets results, not positive thinking.

We should look at ourselves as vessels that need filling up with goodness and light on a daily basis. We have to throw away our old selves and our old habits in order to achieve what we want to be. We must believe in ourselves daily. We must believe that there is a better life waiting for us all, but that only we can create it.

As the old saying goes: "Whether you think you can or think you can't, you are right."

We must seek out the books, the information the people and the knowledge that will help us to do what we want to do. We need to throw away the thoughts and people of old who try to hold us back from becoming the people we want to be.

When we start to move forwards inch by inch, it eventually snowballs and we will travel so fast that nothing negative will be able to cling to us.

The journey for you starts now! Don't wait! We don't know how long we have left on this spinning globe that hangs in the darkness.

What we can do every day is look up into the sky and see the sun that bathes us in light and gives us life. And know this: there is always hope; there is always a different path. You only have to do one thing: take that path and start the journey now.

Be the key to your own future.

Remember: Rather than forgetting about the past, learn from it. What is done is done. We cannot change it. Instead, look to the future, walk towards the light, bathe in its warmth and be the person you deserve to be.

Be who you want to be
We all go through massively emotional times and some very dark times. Surround yourself with positive people and positive energy. If people don't like what you say or do, they are not the people you should be surrounding yourself with. Don't hate them for it, just move along. Try to fill yourself with positive energy from positive people and do the things that make you feel energised and happy. Find a release for all the pains of the past and learn to let it go.

I'm always writing stuff down and deleting it just to give me the image of it being deleted. I even buy those lanterns and write all my bad thoughts, feelings and angers on them, then light them and watch those troubles float away. There is too much hate in this world; too much pain and destruction.

Confrontation is everywhere, and for what? Mostly for self-gratification and ego boosts. Let the ego go and do what makes you happy. Don't worry about what others think. If you want to write, write. If you want to dance, dance. If you want to sing, then sing. And if others call you down for being what you want to be, don't worry about it!

Remember: What people say about you actually says more about them than it does about you. Be positive, live your life with good intentions, help others and be the person you really want to be.

Your Thoughts

Out of the Darkness

Sometimes we all succumb to the darkness. Darkness manifests itself in many different forms, but all of these forms bring with them pain, fear, heartbreak, anguish, anxiety and deep-seated sadness. Sometimes they even bring with them the pinnacle of all darkness: hate! All these feelings can and will, if fed, create procrastination.

Procrastination is a lack of drive born from self-loathing; the mother of hate. Procrastination is an underhand emotion that leads us to believe that the achievements we seek are far from our grasp. Its one aim is to steer us away from our goals and onto a path of failure. When procrastination takes root within the soul it eats away at our dreams and aspirations.

Procrastination feeds on our interests and slowly, one by one, takes them from us, leaving us as shadows of our former selves. A man whose life was once an expanding, living mini-universe fuelled by the drive and determination to achieve his goals suddenly becomes a desolate desert of loss and anguish. Gone are the great days of glory and success, and in their wake lays self-pity and heartbreak.

Recently I have experienced all of these emotions and have spent many dark nights in the company of procrastination, wallowing in self-pity and almost drowning in a sea of sadness. My days have been unproductive and my evenings have been shrouded in darkness. Fear and jealousy, along with hate and deep-rooted sadness, have been my associates.

Lately, when the shroud of blackness has fallen, I have let myself be drawn by the darkness into a paranoid world of self-loathing. My goals and aspirations have been thrown to one side to make way for procrastination.

Outside in the dark I sought my solitude in an alleyway next to my house.

19

I had invited loneliness to become my friend once again. Sitting in the darkness of the alleyway, looking into its blackness, I would blame the world and everyone in it for the wretched despondency I was feeling. Each night I sat waiting for the answer; for a way out of the confusing mess I had got myself into.

One night, very recently, it came. When I sat in the institution of darkness in which I had imprisoned myself, I always sat looking into the darkness and at the end of it stood a cold, lifeless brick wall. Sick of counting out the bricks and staring into a soulless black tunnel capped by the daunting site of the wall, I turned.

And as I turned I noticed the streetlight shining majestically against the cold blackness of the sky. The street lamp lit up the night sky and acted as a beacon of hope against a backdrop of dark, rain-filled clouds. As I sat there, mesmerised by the light, the answer to my predicament came to me and, like a having a dark veil lifted from before my eyes, it filled me with hope.

I had for the previous few weeks been shrouded in a cloak of darkness and my nightly sojourn into the alleyway had taken me into the deceiving arms of self-loathing and procrastination.
Every night as I sat there manifesting my own and many others' downfall I had been trapped in a tunnel of self-pity and fear, but this night I had come to realise what was taking me deeper into the abyss.

Instead of looking out into the light and finding the answers to my problems, I had been looking at the wrong end of this tunnel of disbelief and heartbreak. The whole time I had been courting the shadows; I had been seduced by the blackness that was causing me so much pain. I stood up and walked towards the light of the street lamp that had cut through the darkness and reignited my soul, and with it my inner belief.

21

The light at the end of the tunnel reminded me of some of the dark days of the past and how, in that past, my life had spiralled into a world full of darkness and pain. It reminded me never to look for answers in dark places, but instead to look for the places that harness the light.

Go to the people who shun the darkness and feed on the light. Cast aside the shadows cast by people who live in the seedy world of the night traveller and succumb to its offerings. These pleasures are merely short-lived fun and laughter that is lived out by those who build their lives on sugar pedestals, which will one day crumble and leave them lying in the dark, just as you once did.

Seek out those who will guide you towards the light. You will find these shepherds of light have also walked long and dark paths, and that they now wait for people like you and me to come calling. They wait in patience, knowing that you will arrive. They know the anguish you have felt, for they have felt it themselves. They wait like stonemasons with a tool and chisel, ready to carve you into a warrior of life. They have only one aim in life and that is to bring you out of the darkness and into the light.

Who are these shepherds that lie in wait for you to call?

They are the champions of the dark. They are men and women who have conquered their fears; who have been deep into the darkness, have come out the other side and are now constantly bathed in light.

They are those that inspire. They are trainers and coaches; writers and poets; scientists and teachers; movie makers and preachers. They are the people we want to be, the ones who have made it, and they are waiting for you to seek them out.

Remember: You need to turn around and look out of the darkness and into the light, for it is the light that holds the key to your happiness and success.

Your Thoughts

The Joker in the Pack

Since the dawn of time, man has created social groups. These groups or 'packs' consist of many different characters. From our early school years, through young adulthood and on into our later years, we all have that special group/pack we choose to spend our time with: the best friend from school; the old enemy who is now our closest ally; the next-door neighbour; or perhaps people we have met through friends, who have now become our own close friends.

This pack is nearly always made up of the same recognisable characters. There is always a leader. This person is the rock; the one to be looked up to; the protector of the pack. Then there's the confidante; the one we turn to in times of need or despair. There is always a successful one; one who can't seem to put a foot wrong, whether in business or in their private lives. These people usually drive the fastest cars, have palaces for homes, have found the perfect partner and are seemingly living the perfect life.

Next, depending on whether the pack we belong to is male or female, there is the beautiful or the handsome one. This is the one who attracts more attention from the opposite sex than the rest of the group put together. He or she can't or doesn't want to settle down because life's just too good and waking up with a different partner each week is, as they put it, "all part of the game".

Then there's the one we all feel sorry for. We won't say that out loud, of course, or let them know, although they usually do. They are the ones who may not be the best looking in the pack or have, in the past, been bullied or mistreated before finding the protection of the pack that now surrounds them. They are the ones we feel the need to protect, and we will do so at any cost.

And finally, there is the joker in the pack. He or she is always the first one in the bar and the last one to leave; the first one on the dance floor and the last one off it. The joker is the one who dares to go the furthest and is always ready to entertain. The joker drinks the most shots and dares to try the strongest drinks. Jokers do the most outrageous stunts and are always ready to shock!

Everyone loves the joker in the pack, or so it seems…

The pack knows that the joker doesn't care about anything. I mean, how could he/she? Jokers are always willing to do the things the others in the pack dare not or will not do.

Sometimes, though, the joker tries so hard to entertain the pack that, like the record that once made us dance and brought happiness, he or she now only brings irritation and embarrassment.

The pack invites the joker along for the entertainment value, but eventually, without even realising it themselves, they start to plot in secret. No longer entertained, they revel in the consistent downfall of the joker and, after plying the joker with a few drinks for their own entertainment, the pack ridicules and eggs on the joker so that he or she falls further into the pit of folly.

While the joker continues to play the game, smiling and laughing, the rest of the pack mock and distance themselves further and further, waiting and watching to see just how far the joker will go.

What those in the pack don't realise is, they are not the only ones thinking this. The joker knows; the joker has always known. Jokers know how the other members of the pack feel about them. They understand their role, and they even play up to it. They know their place within the pack and they accept it. And I'll tell you why.

The joker is usually the dreamer of dreams that never quite come to fruition. The jokers are the ones who are carrying

the greatest weight on their shoulders, the most pain in their hearts and the most anguish in their souls.
Secretly they are tired; tired of being Miss or Mr Understood.

Deep inside the joker lies another person: the depressed and worried underachiever who is crying out for attention. The joker yearns to be wanted, to be loved and to be understood.

On their nightly sojourns home, which are usually fairly lonely, they wonder how they keep making the same mistakes over and over again. They long to be just like the others in the pack. They crave to be the quiet one who sits and listens instead of blurting out – usually at the expense of someone else's feelings – the first thought that comes into their heads. They are trapped in a lonely world of needs that they wish they didn't have. Inside, they desperately seek the approval of the pack, searching for the affirmation and attention they think they need to survive and wishing that they could rid themselves of the inner torment they've suffered their whole lives.

The joker in the pack lives behind a painted smile. Jokers are hoping, praying and screaming out in a silent voice for someone to see through the comedy veils they wear and discover the person they really want to be; maybe someone just like you.

How do I know? Because I was once the joker in the pack.

Look at your group of friends and ask yourself, who is our joker? What can I do to lift the comedy veil and tell them that the last curtain call has come, that the show's over and it's time for them to be who they were created to be?

Who is it that needs your true love and attention? Just five minutes of your time could help to free them from years of self-doubt and loathing; to save them from the shows they never really wanted to star in.

Take a look and see if you can find
the joker in your pack. And if you
can't… maybe it's you!

Remember: We all need to take care
of each other and ourselves.

Your Thoughts

The Darkness Never Outshines the Light

Every time I write something of worth I suffer. I suffer a deep pain inside. I feel like I'm living every second of what I'm putting down on the page. Intense depression follows and I fall into a dark pit of despair. It's like I'm shrouded in darkness; a deep, black, intense darkness.

I don't run, I don't hide. I sit in the darkness and just be, knowing that soon I will emerge. In the darkness I learn, and when the learning is done – in the blinking of an eye, like the wind blowing the sand across the desert – the darkness lifts and, like a bug from a cocoon, I rise into a brightness I have never experienced before.

The brightness shines and I see new and beautiful things in the world. It's as though my eyes have been opened a little more than before. I walk in this light and explore the brightness of the new world. I discover, I learn, and then when I have gained knowledge I am once more taken by the darkness to learn my next lesson.

Remember: Every time we enter these dark days there will be pain and there will be sadness, but don't run and don't hide. Go through the darkness and into the light.

Believe and achieve
Someone recently asked me: "How do I achieve?"

My reply was: "You have to believe."

You see, in order to achieve anything, you first have to believe that it's attainable, even if it seems impossible at first. The world is full of once impossible things and impossible dreams.

Just take a look before your very eyes right now. I mean, who would have thought in 1950 (just sixty-four years ago) that one person could talk to the world by typing on a keyboard, which is attached to a screen, which is perched on a lap, which is connected to the world via a network of satellites that float in space, and that these satellites would beam the information around the planet to people thousands of miles apart. Yes, I think that if you had said that sixty years ago people probably would have called you mad. Yet here I am doing exactly that.

Impossible is not a word that should daunt you. Impossible is a word that should drive you. Impossible should inspire you to achieve great things.

Granted, there are some impossible things… for now. But there have been impossible things before now and those things are actually real today. They have been plucked out of time and space and realised; realised by people who hear the word impossible and refuse to accept it. These people then start a journey of manifestation. This journey may take years and years, but ultimately it leads to fruition. If not now, then someday, but eventually it will happen.

The one thing I have noticed about such people – the achievers – is their tenacity, their never-give-up attitudes, their belief that they can attain their goals no matter what. No matter how hard it gets, they press on.

They go through major struggles and hardships, they meet obstacles that at first seem insurmountable, but still they press on. One by one their struggles get easier, their hardships become softer and the insurmountable obstacles are ground down into nothing but dust, which they trample under the feet of success.

Remember: Belief in oneself is a major factor in driving forwards and realising our dreams, but I also believe it is our belief in what makes the universe tick that is the major driving force behind every successful person on the planet.

What is success?

- Success is about achieving one thing, or many things you have set out to achieve
- Success is when you desire something and then attain it
- Success is when our dreams become reality
- Success is when you make the seemingly impossible possible

Just about every successful person I have ever met – and I have met a few – have told me how they struggled, how at times they were brought to their knees, how they almost lost everything, and how they worked so hard that their fingers bled, their minds and bodies were torn or their relationships were strained or broken beyond repair. Every single one of them has told me how close they came to giving up.

In those times of pain, hurt and darkness on the way to success, there is one clear thread that connects them all. Every one of them realised that at the point that they were nearly broken, at the point when they were shrouded in darkness, they reached out. Sometimes they even screamed out, but all of them reached out into the vastness of space and time and called out to a higher power; a power greater than themselves.

Some call this power the universe, some call it nature and others even call it God, but no matter what they call it, they all asked for an intervention. Whether it was divine or not (I like to think that it was), each of them got the intervention that ultimately led them to achieve their success.

When I started out on my journey towards achievement, I learnt many lessons, just like these people. Many of these lessons were serendipitous (happy accidents), or so I thought. Until I looked back on the things I have achieved so far, that was.

In less than twelve years, I went from being a completely depressed, uneducated, fighting jobless drunk, to a man who holds a Bachelor of Science degree, is a published author (see my book, *The Twelve-Step Warrior*) a scriptwriter, a filmmaker and a drunk that has been sober for thirteen years. And, although it has taken me all my life to be able to say this and believe it… I am a good man.

During this process, I had to believe that there was something out there that could help. I had to stop believing that I was the centre of the universe. I had to understand that I don't hold all the answers, that I don't know what makes the universe tick and that I certainly can't control it.

It was only then that I started to achieve success. Now let me just say this. My success is NOT ruled by how much I earn, but rather by how much I achieve.

I have always said: "Never measure your own success by someone else's achievements."

I aimed to get a degree because I was sick of being an uneducated man. It pained me when I thought back to the old school reports I received (when I was there, that is), which always ended with the words 'Could have done better'. I hated them until I realised that it was those thoughts and those comments that were the driving force behind my success. Failure wasn't my downfall; failure became my saving grace.

I learnt how to achieve through my lessons; the lessons I learnt on the way to success; the ones that brought me to my knees and shrouded me in darkness. These lessons are valuable, and the place they bring you to – that place of realisation, that place where you find yourself screaming out into the universe, to God – that place is essential. That place is the place where we find our moment of belief.

That moment when our prayers are answered leads us to faith: a faith in a higher power; a faith in something bigger than ourselves; a faith in God; a faith that we can achieve our greatest dreams; a faith that we can attain the impossible; a faith that leads us to knowing that… **if we believe, we can achieve!**

Remember: Belief is essential if you want to succeed.

Your Thoughts

Reward Yourself Properly

Do you reward yourself? Believe it or not, a lot of people don't reward themselves enough and the ones that do often give themselves false rewards.

Let me explain. I know a lot of people who work hard day after day. They are either working towards their dreams in one creative field or another, or are simply working to survive, but either way they rarely give themselves the right rewards.

What are rewards?
The most common type of reward is the yearly holiday. Every year, millions of us travel to distant shores for our yearly break. This one big reward signifies the end of a year of hard work. We say to ourselves: "I've worked hard all year, I deserve a break". And guess what? You do!

This yearly reward is a much-needed time to let ourselves go and enjoy ourselves without the hindrance of the daily grind, and by the end of it we should be relaxed and energised enough to come back all guns blazing, ready once more to attack the path that leads to the realisation of our dreams.

The truth, though, is that most of us go away and reward ourselves so much that we need a holiday to get over the one we just had! So the question is, do we reward ourselves in ways that benefit us and our goals?

The more I speak to people about this, the more I find that as a working nation we don't reward ourselves with the right type of rewards, and by that I mean rewards that may actually not be a rewards at all!

More and more people reward themselves by having an alcoholic drink at the end of the day, and there's nothing wrong with that. If that's what people choose to do, who am I to say that having a drink after a hard day's work is wrong?

But what I will say is this: if you reward yourself with an alcoholic drink every night, that will eventually become a problem. Rather than being a reward, it will start to be a hindrance. The daily routine of working hard all day and drinking every night will eventually take its toll. Probably without even realising it, you would become dependent on that drink to get you through the night.

Some nights you might consume more than you actually wanted to and you might even start to end up drunk on a regular basis. This, in turn, could lead to you missing work the next day which, again, will affect the outcome of your work. In some cases it might lead to you losing your job. In the long term, your reward has turned into your downfall.

Let's say you're on a diet, you're heading towards your goal and are achieving your weight loss more quickly than you expected. You may choose to give yourself a small reward, a chocolate bar, maybe. No harm done… at first! That is, until the rewards start to become more and more frequent, and eventually you've given yourself so many rewards (of the chocolate kind) that you're no longer on your diet at all.

Now don't get me wrong. I'm not saying that we shouldn't have rewards for our efforts, but what I am saying is, let's make these rewards beneficial to our work and our dreams.

Instead of the nightly glass of wine or beer, why not reward your hard day's work with an extra hour of sleep by turning in early, or an extra-long soak in the tub with that book you've been longing to read, or sitting back and putting on that new album you've just bought and really appreciating it, instead of it just being on in the background while you're concentrating on other things.

If you're on a diet, make sure your treat is something that is beneficial to the diet. Maybe treat yourself by trying out a new exercise class, but instead of it being hard work, make it something adventurous, something exciting or something relaxing; something you wouldn't normally do. Yoga, maybe, or tai chi. Or a nice relaxing spa evening or that aromatherapy massage you've been promising yourself.

One thing about all of the suggestions above is, they all come guilt free!
You see, we need balance in our rewards. We need to make our rewards reflect our hard work.

Our rewards should support our journeys, not pushing us away from them! So next time you reward yourself for a job well done, make it a real reward; a reward that will benefit you and help you on the way to your goal.

There are times when we feel like our goals are just too far away and that giving up is easier. Do NOT fall into this trap! That's all it is: a trap that has been set in your way to try and stop you on your journey to glory. It is a test that has been put in place to see whether you are worthy of the goal you are striving so hard to attain.

Remember: NEVER give up! Instead, give yourself a reward, but make that reward beneficial to your goal and enjoy it. We are on the journey for a short time, but our final destinations will last forever.

Your Thoughts

Nothing to do

I hear a lot of people these days saying that they're bored or have nothing to do.

I remember years ago, during my dark days, when I would stay in bed until 2pm and wake to my first cigarette, which I would ignite within seconds of opening my eyes. While leaning back on my bed, looking around my small, box-room flat, I would think about what I could do to fill my time until I got to my night-time job in the bar or the club.

Back then my life was upside down and I did my most of my 'living' (or what I thought was living) during the night. I would lie there thinking about what I could do all day to keep me occupied or listing the things I needed to do; in fact, I thought that long and hard about it that I didn't get anything done. I had become a professional procrastinator.

I rarely did anything I said was going to do!

Procrastination: "The act of procrastinating; putting off or delaying or deferring an action to a later time."

Procrastination is the killer of dreams; the eternal excuse; the ultimate friend of tomorrow; a tomorrow that never comes.

These days for me are quite different. Now when I wake up I can't get out of bed quickly enough. In fact, most nights I spend so much time creating that sleep eludes me (which is not a good thing and it's something I'm working on and getting better at, but that's for another blog).

Every day now I get up, I have my morning cup of tea and then I write. I love writing. It helps me get rid of any crap I have built up inside and is playing on my mind. I love creating something out of nothing.

Just lately, more and more people are telling me that my writing has helped them, and I want writing and directing to be my full-time job. Practice makes perfect and I am certainly not perfect.

After my morning writing session I eat or go for a walk in Loughborough, where I live, and I see family or friends. I love going to see my friend Jay. We sit on a bench in town and that's where I get my inspiration for characters or stories.

I love to 'people watch'. You can learn a lot from people watching: the way people talk, the way they walk, their many different mannerisms; the overheard snippets of conversation that melt into one another, giving nothing but inspiration and ideas for my next piece of writing.

After sitting with Jay for a while, I head home and note down the snippets of conversations and characters that have caught my eye. It's a file I can turn to when writing my scripts; my bank account of people, places and things from which I can make a withdrawal whenever I'm trying to find a voice for a character, story or script I am writing.

In total, I have written approximately eighty different scripts, short stories, plays and treatments (the storyline of a film).

This is my bank account of work for when I make it big! We all want to make it big, right? I write all the time now, and after I have written I give myself a small reward, as mentioned above. When I write I feel alive. I feel relaxed and I feel like I have that sense of achievement we all need.

I don't procrastinate these days; I make lists. I make a list of everything I want to do that day and I do it, marking it off the list as I go. I mark it off the list so that I get that sense of satisfaction you get when something is achieved. I love that feeling of achievement. You can't beat achieving the goals you set yourself. Whether they are hourly, daily, monthly or yearly ones, they all feel good.

One of my goals is to win a BAFTA, and I'm working towards that goal every second of every day. Every time I sit down to write, every time I go out and make a film, every time I send an email hoping to get my big break, it's on my mind in everything I do.

What I'm trying to say is that I don't know how people – and mostly it's the people that have the biggest goals and the greatest dreams – find the time to have nothing to do!

If you have a goal, don't procrastinate. Work towards it. Think about it every waking second. Ask yourself:

1. How can I achieve that goal?
2. What is it going to take to get there?
3. What can you do in those times of being bored or having nothing to do to inch yourself closer to that goal?
4. Do it!
5. Do it some more!
6. See points four and five

I recently started to write up my new book, *The Temple*, but it has taken me about a year of planning to get it to this stage; the stage at which I'm happy to finally give it some structure and format it into the story I want to tell.

Some people will scoff and say: "Here is a man who is telling us not to procrastinate, but it takes him a year to prepare a book." And if I didn't know what the processes of writing a book were and the length of time it takes to write one, I would agree. But to write a book or achieve a dream you have to have solid foundations. You can't build a house before you've laid the foundations, or that house will fall.

The book I'm writing is about a very sensitive issue that affects everyone I know at some point or another, so it's important for me to get the foundation and the research right. That takes time and hard work, and there is no room for procrastination. If I want it to be right I have to do the work.

I am currently working on a feature film script, three short film scripts, two books, prepping to shoot another film, creating a business plan for my new business (which is not easy for me), creating a website for that business and preparing a marketing strategy to get that business recognised so that I can make a success of it.

That success will give me an income I can use to practise my craft and to make more films. That, in turn, will push me to achieve more and more, and hopefully along the way I can inspire others do to the same. Ultimately, I hope to achieve one of my long-term goals. I want to win a BAFTA and I will.

It's hard work, but I love it because I know it will all pay off. It will all come to fruition. It cannot fail to as long as I do the work.

No, procrastination is not for me. Creation, however, is.

Go create, go and achieve your goals, inch your way towards your dreams.

Remember: When you have nothing to do, DO SOMETHING!

Your Thoughts

Thank F*ck it's Friday

Thank f*ck it's Friday! I hear that phrase bantered around all the time. Thank f*ck it's the end of the week! Thank f*ck the weekend is here!

I get it, I definitely get it. You've worked hard all week, and now you get a couple of days to spend with your family, do the things you love or just relax and take some time for yourself. And why not? You've earned it.

I used to wake up every morning and fear the day. In fact, I feared everything. I feared the morning, the daily hangovers and the dry retching I woke to. I feared the day that I would spend promising myself I would never hit the bottle again. I feared the night and my battle with temptation, and I feared the copious amounts of alcohol I would eventually consume (usually at someone else's expense) after temptation had won once again. I lived in fear every day of every week. Except Friday, that is. On Fridays I came alive!

On Friday nights back in the 1990s I was a DJ at a local bar and nightclub. I played house music and I loved it. I wasn't the best DJ in the world, and the club was no Paradise Garage, but it was on a Friday that I was set free. Yes, I still drank and yes, I would still suffer the same dry retching hangovers in the morning, but Fridays were different for me. It was when the fear dissipated and I was set free.

Standing there in the DJ box getting lost in the music was a time of peace. It was my time of freedom, whether people knew it or not, when I got to set my emotions free through my music. I looked forward to Friday more than any other day of the week.

The thing is, I wanted to have that Friday feeling every day of the week. I yearned for it on a daily basis, that feeling of freedom, that feeling of deep-seated happiness that I prayed for.

And guess what? Now, I have it!

Everyday feels like a Friday now. I am blessed. Every day I'm doing what I always wanted to do. I write, I work towards making films and I spend time with my beautiful children. I have my problems, but everybody does, right? I miss my children when they're not with me, I sometimes even feel a few regrets, but I no longer attend the pity parties of old.

I wake up, I have my thoughts, and then I deal with them. I say my morning prayer: "God grant me the serenity to accept the things I cannot change, the courage to change the things I can and the wisdom to know the difference."

Then I have my morning cup of tea and reflect on all the beautiful things I have in my life and all the great people I know; great people like you!

Then, happy to be alive and happy to be living a life that is blessed, I say to myself: "Thank f*ck it's Friday or Saturday or Sunday or Monday or Tuesday or Wednesday or Thursday!"

Yes! Every day is a Friday when you love the life you lead and the people you live it alongside.

Remember: It's a simple plan. If you're happy, keep going. And if you're not, change it! NOW!

Your Thoughts

Tears in the Night

This morning I woke up crying. I woke up in tears; those uncontrollable, sobbing tears that start deep down in your heart and flow like they are rising from a pool of sadness that is trapped deep in the recesses of your heart.

I don't know the reason; in fact, I don't think there was one. I just think that, while sleeping, I connected with something from my past that saddened me. It was nothing in particular, just a random memory that had risen to the top of the memory pool.

I have many memories, as we all do: memories of times I regret; memories of old friends that I no longer see; memories of friends that have long since passed but have left an imprint on my heart; memories of relationships that held happiness and sadness in equal measure; embarrassing memories, sad memories;

and memories of people I loved (and still do), but are no longer with me in this world.

I assume that while I was asleep, one or maybe more of these memories was accessed and brought to the forefront of my mind, instigating the tears that fell.

I sat for a moment when I woke up and cried. I didn't try to stop it; I just let the tears flood out. I sat and thought deeply about what had made me cry, trying to connect to a long gone dream. I saw fleeting images of the dream I had had the night before, but nothing stuck.

The images slipped away every time I tried to grasp one. I was like an oily-handed man catching eels in the rain. I sat for a while and just cried. I let the process of letting go work its magic through me.

I understand now that when I cry I'm letting go; letting go of the sadness these memories bring and being filled with joy instead of succumbing a deep depression. You see, I know that as long as I have these emotions flowing through my mind, body and spirit, I am alive. I understand that while I am on this short sojourn through life I will lose people I love, and inevitably I will lose people that I think I cannot live without, or they will lose me. Very depressing, you might think, but alas, that is the way of the world we live in. It's the circle of life.

It is also inevitable that I will create more memories, and that some memories will be created for me by the people I meet, the friends I make and the people I love, and that these memories will shape my future dreams.

So how do I stop the tears in the night?

In order to make my future dreams the happiest dreams I could have, I need to do a few things. I have to create fantastic future memories; memories that will fuel my future dreams.

I know that if I surround myself with positive people – people who have dreams that I can believe in, and the kind that encourage and believe in me – I cannot go wrong.

The people I mix with, the places I go and the memories I create will bring joy to my present and my future dreams.

These days I am careful in choosing my influences. I am mindful of the company I keep and the friends I have. I no longer surround myself with those that seek to bring me down or throw the sands of doubt in my face. No, those people are not for me.

Through many tears and much sadness I have let go of the people, the past hates and the anger that used to create my memories and my dreams. I have replaced them with hope, opportunity and people that fuel me. I have let go of the old friends that spoke good to my face and ill behind my back.

Those people are not my friends. The chaff has been separated from the wheat.

These days, if you're in my company, the chances are you inspire me, you make me happy; you're helping me create my future memories, my future happiness and my future dreams. You take away the tears in the night.

Remember: It's good to own our emotions and understand that they are part of the process; part of the circle of life. They are not there to keep us in pain, but to lead us to freedom.

Your Thoughts

Doing the Do

I knew a man once who seemed to have read every book in the world. He knew everything, but he read so much chasing the wisdom he sought that he never had the time to do anything, and he died full of regret.

It's OK to have knowledge, but without action it is nothing. You can chase knowledge all your life and die an unwise man, for real knowledge and wisdom do not come from the pages of a book. Genuine wisdom comes from experience.

There is a line in the film *Good Will Hunting* where Robin Williams says to Matt Damon: "I bet you could read a book in a day and tell me about all the works of Michelangelo, but the sad thing is you can't tell me what it smells like in the Sistine Chapel" (or words to that effect).

What Robin Williams is basically saying to him is: it's ok to know something or have knowledge about that thing, but you will never really know that thing until you have experienced it first hand: what it smells like, how it feels. Experiencing 'it' (whatever 'it' may be) gives you great insight. Just knowing about something doesn't give you any insight at all.

Many of us have dreams and aspirations of achieving great things and some of us are heading towards these dreams, but some are moving towards them faster than others.

The ones that are in front are the ones who are out there already becoming what they want to be, not the ones who are sitting and talking about what they want to be. Action, they say, speaks louder than words.

So if you're dreaming about making that film or writing that book or climbing that mountain or running that marathon, don't sit around wasting your valuable time talking about it and planning it and putting it off until tomorrow, because tomorrow never comes.

Get out there and start doing what it is you want to do: now, today!

If you want to be a filmmaker, start filming, if you want to write that novel, go get a pen and paper or your laptop and start writing it. You'll find that the wisdom you seek and the glory of achievement is in the doing not in the thinking of doing, or in the planning of doing.

Remember: The more doing you do, the more you'll get done.

Your Thoughts

It's Never About the Money!

We need money to survive in this world, that's the way it is. We need to buy food, we need to pay our bills and we are hard-pressed to find anything in this day and age that doesn't cost us something. But how do we get to the stage where we can make good money and carve out a decent living?

I write a lot. I have written two books up until now and one of them was published by a very well-known publishing company. I have made two short films and scripts, edited a few more and made corporate videos for some of the biggest companies in the UK.

But the question is, do I make much money? And the answer is simple: NO, I don't!

So why do I continue to write? Why do I continue to make films? And why do

I write my daily blog? I do it because I love it and I have a passion for it.

It took me five years of getting into debt, five years of sacrifice and five years of not giving up for me to earn my degree, and believe me I earned it! It cost me thousands of pounds and thousands of hours to attain the skills I needed to do what I love. To be able to wake every day and do what I love, create the things I want to create and be surrounded by the people I want to be surrounded by. Of course, it would be better if I was earning a living from it, too, but the fact is I'm not.

So why don't I give up?

I don't give up, because I know it is the love and passion for what I do that drives me in the creation of the things I do. I don't have my eye on the money, and when I do something I never think about how much I can earn. I do it because I love what I do.

When I do something without the money in mind, that something – whether it be a book, an article or a film – usually turns out to be a fantastic product. It turns out this way because I put my all into everything I create.

When I wrote *The Twelve-Step Warrior*, I have to admit that I did it for myself. I did it to get rid of all the years of heartache and pain I had suffered and carried around inside of me, which was weighing me down like a sack of stinking shit! I was sick of the pain and the heartache. I was sick of carrying around all those years of shame and guilt for the troubles I had caused and the people I had hurt.

I created that book by putting in hours of valuable time, heartache and pain. I cried tears into every page and regurgitated memories I didn't want to live through again. I deleted it, left it and binned it, but eventually I came back to it and finished it. I had to. I had to get rid of my shit!

Yes, it was a very selfish reason, but the upside was that not only did I get rid of my shit; that book is now out there in the world, helping to get rid of other people's shit, too.

I have received hundreds of thank you messages. People message me or call me every day asking me if I can help them through their shit, whatever it may be. And if I can, I do.

I have to. I have to be there for others as they were there for me. I could name hundreds of people who have helped me both financially and emotionally since my recovery. So I am in a position (albeit not financially yet) to help in many other ways, whether it is being a shoulder to cry on, providing a piece of friendly advice or just offering an open ear. I am here, and if I can help I will.

I once promised a man that I would one day pay for him to go to Disney World. This guy had helped me in ways you wouldn't believe. He was there for me in dark times and he helped me out financially, but most of all he was an open ear, a shoulder to cry on and a very good friend.

I am not (yet) in a position where I can fulfil that promise, but every day it's on my mind. However, I still don't do what I do for the money. I do it because I love it and I'm passionate about what I do.

But here's the payoff. If I do what I do every day, I get better at it. The books I write and the films I make get better and better. The quality goes up and the product becomes more desirable. And when a product is desirable, people will pay.

The truth is, people want the best. They want something that has heart and soul embedded in it, and when that happens, it shows. People start to take notice of what it is you do, and the work you do becomes 'in demand'. When there is demand for your work, the financial rewards will come. But you will not get that quality, your work will not be in demand and financially you will be left in the fiscal desert if the thing you are concentrating on is money.

So whatever it is you do, do it for the love. Do it for the passion, do it to help others, do it because you would do it for free. That way, what you produce will be the best product on the market, people will take note and financial rewards will eventually come to you.

Every successful person I have ever met who was cash rich did it from their hearts. They followed their dreams and they worked their asses off in the process and, eventually, after a lot of time and sacrifice, the money found them. But even in the cases where it hasn't happened (yet), they are happy people, because every day they wake up and look forward to doing the things they love, the things they are passionate about. They are living their dreams.

Remember: It's better to be rich in life before you become rich in money!

Your Thoughts

Audi do That?

A few months ago, while stuck in a rut, I was walking along the high street in Loughborough when I passed a man getting out of an Audi R8.

The Audi R8 is one awesome car, I love it. Sure, there may be other cars out there that carry more prestige, but for me the Audi R8 is a beautiful-looking machine. I stopped to admire the beautiful machine that stood in front of me. Then the driver got out.

I immediately said to him: "Well done, mate, that's an awesome car."

The driver had an obvious look of shock on his face and literally sighed at my comment. "What, really?" he said.

I replied: "Of course really. Why not really?"

He stood next to me, looking at the car, and said: "Thanks mate. That really means a lot to me."

I was surprised by his comment and asked why he gave me such a reply.

The driver turned to me and said: "Well, normally I get a comment like, 'Flash twat!' or 'Lucky bastard'." Then he told me how he came to own this majestic beauty of the road.

"I worked my ass of for this car, you know. I dreamt for years about owning a car like this. I built my own business from nothing and I really worked hard. I was skint for years, then all of a sudden my business took off and bam! I made a million in what seemed to others like it was overnight. But what they didn't know was how long and how hard I worked for it."

The driver of the car was nearly in tears. He continued: "I mortgaged my house and nearly lost everything I owned. I worked my fingers to the bone, but people don't see that, do they?"

I looked at him and said: "Thank you, mate."

He asked me what for, to which I replied: "Because you telling me that lets me know that it's possible for me to achieve my dreams, too."

We are often too quick to judge others, whether it's because of what they have or what they haven't got. We often make judgements about people's characters before we know their stories.

Remember: The harder you work, the more successful you will be!

Your Thoughts

Acceptance: The Mother of all Change

Life goes on. Day after day we experience change. Change is inevitable, because if there was no change we would get stuck in a mundane world of the never never. Life would become dull, boring and hard to face.

All of us will experience trauma and loss in our lives: loss of relationships, loss of friends, loss of the ones we love and trauma from the memories of events in our lives that we would rather forget.

Loss and trauma can be triggered by many different things. Some we can control and others we can't. Sometimes these traumas and losses are so big they change our lifestyles to such an extent that we cannot see past the next day, the next hour or even the next second. Life becomes a struggle; it becomes painful. Some days when we wake up we just want to put our heads back under the sheets and shut ourselves away from the world outside.

Inside, we know that this is not the way forward. We know this is not going to change the traumas and losses we are dealing with, but sometimes it seems like the only choice we have.

Let me tell you now that there is another way; a way that leads us out of the darkness and into a newer, brighter future. That way is acceptance.

The trouble is, the path to acceptance is a long and dark road. This road is fraught with dark days and lonely nights; it is fraught with pain and heartache, confusion and rivers of tears. But don't worry. These pains, these dark days, these lonely nights and emotions are part of the process we must go through in order to reach the place where we experience acceptance.

We have to embrace these processes and understand that they are not designed to kill us. They are designed to help us through our traumas and losses, and they lead to acceptance.

We have to look at the way we feel and tell ourselves: "Of course I feel this way, why wouldn't I? Look what has happened. I have lost the one I love, I have experienced a trauma in my life that is hard to face and what I'm feeling is normal."

Don't worry if, after your losses or traumas, the path becomes harder, the road through life takes an uphill turn and the way forward seems to be blocked at every turn, because these things are leading us to acceptance.

There's an old saying: "These things are sent to try us." But are they? Or are they just a part of life?

It is my belief that the emotions we feel, the dark days we live through, the loneliness and the tears we experience are part of the purification process; a process we have to go through in order to accept the changes that have taken place.

This purification process can help us understand what has happened and why it has happened, giving us time to grieve and eventually accept what has happened before we finally move on.

Accepting and moving on doesn't mean we have to forget the things we have lost. Acceptance simply means that we have dealt with our traumas and our losses. It means that we have had our grieving periods, and that we can continue with life in a way that those we have lost along the way would be proud of. It means that the traumas of our past can no longer hold us to ransom and cut us off from the happiness we all deserve.

Acceptance means that we can live again. We can press on with life with a deeper understanding and we can build new relationships with the people we still have around us, or who are yet to enter our lives. We gain experience from the challenges we have faced, and these can make the challenges we face in the future easier to bear.

We will still feel emotional pain, the sadness will still hurt and the heartache will still cause us to suffer, but we will have a newfound knowledge that we are able to get through. We can live on through the darkness into a better life, into a brighter future; a future where we no longer sit under the black veil of trauma.

I have dealt with many losses and many traumas in my life. Some have been massive and others not so big, but all come with the same emotions attached. Along the way, I have used a few different techniques to let these traumas go and to live a life that the ones I love but are no longer with me are proud to look down on.

I have sent letters to loved ones, letters to the ones I hurt. I take my pen and I write a letter. I write what I want to say to the person; what I need to say. Then I put it in an envelope and do one of two things. If I feel this letter would not cause anyone any harm, either emotionally or physically (I have to know for sure, which I must admit has not been often) I send it. If I'm not sure, I take it and I burn it somewhere very safe. I watch the smoke rise into the sky, taking with it the words I wrote.

1. **Lantern therapy** (I made that name up. It's not a real therapy, but it works for me)
I buy a Chinese lantern or three, depending on how much I have to write. Gently taking care not to rip the lantern, I take a felt tip and write my traumas, emotions, fears, heartaches, worries and pains on them. Then I take them to a quiet place, a special place for me, and I light them. I then watch them float up into the night sky, taking with them my troubles and pain.

2. Bobbing bottles and boats
I have, in the past, written my troubles down on paper, folded them, put them in a bottle and placed them into a fast-running stream and watched them

bob up and down, washing my troubles away. Once I found some origami patterns for boats and made them out of the paper I wrote on and did the same thing.

3. Prayer

I often sit and pray. I pray for forgiveness, I pray for happiness, I pray for love to surround everyone I know and for peace to fill their hearts. I pray for acceptance… and just lately it has arrived.

Remember: Holding on to past hurts will keep you standing still. Dealing with your traumas will set you free, and honouring the people you have lost will allow you to live the life they would want you to lead.

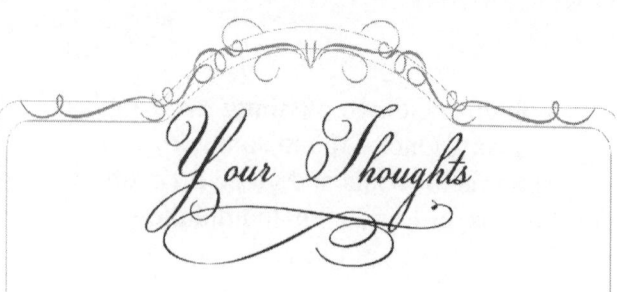
Your Thoughts

Behind a Painted Smile

We look at people and often make assumptions about who they are, what they do and how they live their lives. We deduce all of this from what we see in front of us, but often our assumptions are inaccurate.

Some people present themselves as happy-go-lucky people, always with a smile on their faces, but this is not always the reality. Sometimes the happiest-looking people are hiding the biggest heartbreaks. I am always reminded of the old Motown song "Behind a Painted Smile" when I come across people like this.

These people hold on to past hurts and past memories that hurt them and they cannot let them go. They stumble around blindly, hoping that the past can be preserved in the present. The trouble is, it can't. The past is the past, the present is the present and the future is yet to be created. We can hold on to memories of the past and relive them in our minds, but we cannot have that past back.

I often look back on my life, and I certainly have regrets, but I don't hold on to them. Doing so would only serve to kill the present and the present is all we have.

The present can be full of past hurts and regrets, or it can be something you create on a daily basis. We kill the present and make our futures dark when we hold on to the dark memories of the past.

In order to have a present that is full of joy, we have to let go of our past hurts and concentrate on the things that are good in our lives now. We have to appreciate the now. We have to look to the things that bring us joy and laughter today.

How do we create happy memories?

Well, that's easy. If we enjoy the present, tomorrow we can look back on our yesterdays with a smile and not a tear; with laughter rather than heartache. We build our futures from our presents.

The really good thing about the future is, it isn't here yet and it never will be, whereas the past follows us everywhere we go. So let go of the past and build the future by loving the present. After all, today is a gift: a PRESENT!

Remember: What we do today creates our tomorrows.

Your Thoughts

The Blue Brick

So you get up, you get out of bed
and you find yourself in a foul mood.
You don't know why you're in a mood,
you just are. And guess what? It's
everybody else's fault!

Sometimes we wake up and our
moods are foul. We hate the world and
everyone in it, and we want them to
know it, too. We can't just keep it to
ourselves. We have to make sure that the
people who surround us – mostly the
ones we love the most – know it as well.
We are not satisfied that our own mood
is down; we have to push that mood onto
others. Why is that?

Well, our moods are created by our
influences. What we ingest cerebrally
affects our every thought and feeling.
The good things and the bad things all
affect our mood in some way.

Pushing our moods onto others is a selfish act. Most people believe we cannot change our moods, thoughts and feelings, but we definitely can.

What we have to do is find a way to vent. We have to find a healthy way of changing that mood before it infects the people that surround us. There are many ways to change these moods, but all of them involve one act: venting.

Venting is a way of releasing our emotions. We can cry, we can shout (often at others, who don't deserve it), we can hit the gym, we can talk it through… we can do many things, but it has to come out.

Many creatives, writers, filmmakers, artists, musicians and professional fighters experience depression when they are not creating. When they stop doing what it is they do, they start to hit depression and that depression gets worse until they start practising their art again.

The writer has to write, the artist has to paint, the musician will create and the fighter will train, and when they do they often find that their best work comes out. We need to be vigilant about our cerebral ingestion; we need to be mindful of what we feed our brains. If you sat and ate junk food all day you would get fat, become unhealthy and, ultimately, you would suffer. So why do it to the brain?

Make sure that your mind ingests things that are wholesome and positive. Fill it with images of love and affection; with music and lyrics that make you happy. Make sure that the conversations you have are positive. Mindless gossip about her at work or him at the gym just won't do you any good.

Tackle your problems head on and talk to your partner or best friends about the problems you're having. If they don't want to hear it, they are not your true friends. Find some that are willing to listen and share with you. A problem shared is a problem halved, as they say. Phone up about that bill that is worrying you and make arrangements. You will find that there is a mass of help out there for you, but it's not going to come knocking on your door. You have to start the process.

Clear out all the things that bring you down, and if you're not happy with something, change it. Feed the mind as you would the body. If you put junk in, you'll only get junk (thoughts) out!

Imagine that on your back you carry an invisible rucksack, and every problem or emotion you don't deal with is a heavy blue brick. Every time you fail to deal with that problem or emotion, you have to put that blue brick into your rucksack. The rucksack on your back will get so heavy that it will eventually bring you to your knees.

You may already have a rucksack that is full or half full of blue bricks on your back, painfully weighing you down. Start by emptying that, pulling one brick out at a time and dealing with it. That way it won't have to go back into the rucksack. Work your way through the rucksack, emptying out all the blue bricks, and when your rucksack is empty you will feel lighter, you will feel stronger and you will walk with your head held high. You will be back in control and you will be more mindful of filling it again with the blue bricks. When we feel lighter and brighter, our moods will follow suit.

Your Thoughts

Venting

Find a field or a quiet place and scream! Scream as loud as you can about all the things in the world that bother you. Punch the air and really let go of those bad emotions. They are clogging up the good ones up.

Get creative, write it out, paint it out, make music or go train and run those bad emotions into the ground. They are only blocking the path to the good ones.
Cry, too. There is nothing wrong with a good cry. Crying is a healthy emotion that helps us express ourselves and unclogs us of all the shit that blocks the path to happiness.

Tackle your problems head on, have that conversation, make that phone call, express that feeling, tell people you're not happy with whatever it is and stick to your guns. It's your happiness, and when

you're happy it will infect the people you
surround yourself with.

Remember: We can start the day
again at any time, and others do not need
to suffer from our emotions, our bad
moods and our unnecessary worries.
Smile, it's infectious!

Your Thoughts

The Naysayers

They say it cannot be done. They say you will never do it. They say it's not for you; that it will never last… Well, whoever they are, they can fuck right off!

They are the naysayers. According to urbandictionary.com, the naysayer is:

One who frequently engages in excessive complaining, negative banter and/or a genuinely poor and downbeat attitude. Naysayers are distinguished by their tendency to consistently view the glass as half empty, make frequent one-way trips to negativetown and constantly emphasise the worst of a situation.

Naysayers will consistently tell you that you cannot achieve your dreams; that you cannot do the job you yearn to do; and that you cannot become the person you want to be.

Naysayers are usually the types of people that have given up on their dreams, goals and aspirations because they became too hard, or because more sacrifice than was initially expected was needed. Naysayers believe that because they couldn't do it, you can't do it. They only walk the short path to glory, for the long path is too long a road.

I want to tell you that the naysayers are wrong! You can achieve your goals, you can have the dream job and you can live the life you want to live. Yes, it does take hard work. Yes, it does mean sacrifice, and yes, it will take time, but not as long as the naysayers make out.

Do not, under any circumstances, listen to these people. They are the killers of dreams and the harbourers of negativity. They will shatter your confidence and destroy your determination in one fell swoop. Avoid them like the plague.

Look to surround yourself with those that enthuse you; those that tell you it can be done; the people who get excited when you tell them what you are going to do.

As for the naysayers, use their negatives attitude to fuel your journey on the way to your dreams. Try not to stay long in their company, but understand that they are sneaky little buggers. They will pop up in the most unexpected places and try to bring you down.

When the naysayers tell you it can't be done, don't throw that statement away. Keep it and use it for fuel. Every time you feel like quitting, remember their words. Remember them and let those words energise you. Let their negative shit become the rocket fuel that propels you forwards towards your goals.

Remember: There is one sure way to quieten a naysayer. Simply achieve the things that they say you cannot do.

Your Thoughts

Something Out of Nothing

I am still hearing it: "I have nothing to do." People say it often, but do little about it. The answer is simple, but hard to do, it seems.

There was a time when I would say the same thing over and over and over again; so much so that I got sick of the same sentence going round and round inside my head. Until I found the answer, that was. I have said this before, and I'll say it again: when you've got nothing to do, do something!

We all have things that we choose to put off until tomorrow. Whether they are big or small, we all have unfinished or not yet started things to do. But how much do we really want to do them?

Most of the unfinished things are jobs that seem too tedious or not exciting enough. They are the uninteresting things

that we feel are best left for another day;
a day that hardly ever arrives.

I have found that these things we
have not yet done or are yet to start tend
to be the things that get us down. People
rarely worry about their
accomplishments or the goals they have
reached. No, these seem to be the things
that bring the most joy. Yet thousands of
us say the same thing every day: "I'll do
it tomorrow". We all know the old
saying, "tomorrow never comes", and the
thing is, one day it won't!

Often we hear of people whose lives
are snatched away from under their feet
before they can do the things they wanted
to do. It's a sad fact of life, but
nevertheless it happens every single day.

I now understand that it's not the
things we finish that break us. It is the
things that are left unfinished or that we
never even start. When we say we have
nothing to do, we are just lying to
ourselves. What we really mean is, "I
can't be bothered", "I'm too lazy", "It'll

wait", or even – believe it or not – "It'll sort itself out!" Well, it won't! Action has to be taken. Nothing ever sorts itself out, and that is a fact.

I have found that the most productive thing to do is to make a list of all the unfinished things and another list of all the things I have yet to start. When I complete an unfinished thing, I make a start on one of the yet-to-start things. This way, I always have something to do.

From this I get two things done and a sense of achievement from completing another goal (all the unfinished things should be goals). And I get a sense of excitement about starting something new. I have also found that the things I am not looking forward to doing the most give me the greatest sense of achievement and sometimes spark a new interest for me.

From having the two lists, I have found that there is always something to do.

But think about this… What if doing nothing was on your list? That way, when you came to that section of your list, you would be doing something.

Let me explain. If doing nothing is part of your to do list, you change it from a negative to a positive. Doing nothing becomes something of value that you can look forward to after you have done something.

"Oxymoron! Oxymoron! Oxymoron!" shouts the crowd.

Well, yes and no! But it's a productive oxymoron. By doing nothing, you are actually doing something. If you do nothing in the right way, it can be brilliant. If you do nothing in the wrong way, it can be a pain in the ass and a downright bore.

A planned 'doing nothing' session will consist of nothing at all: no computer, no phone, no noise, no talking. Nothing at all. A planned 'doing nothing' session should be relaxing and should help to recharge your batteries. It will wind you down from all the 'doing somethings' and quiet the mind of all the boringness that so many speak of.

So the next time you have nothing to do, you have a choice. Go to your two lists – the unfinished or the not yet started – and do something… even if it's nothing.

Remember: When you've got nothing to do, DO SOMETHING!

Your Thoughts

The Other You

"The war is constant and the battles are daily, but I can never give up." These are the words at the front of my book, *The Twelve-Step Warrior*. Someone asked me last week what the meaning behind them was. Who is the war against? Do you win every battle?

Let me explain. The war that is constant is the war against the other me, and this was particularly poignant during the early days of recovery.

I was fighting many addictions, the main one being alcoholism, and I felt like every day was a battle. I had to fight the urge to drink one day at a time. In fact, some days I had to fight them one hour, one minute, or even one second at a time. But I found that the older I got in sobriety, the more battles I would win.

I once asked an old stalwart of AA –
a man who had been sober for fifty years
– why I was in a constant battle. Was it
always going to be like this?

His reply came back in a calm but
strong, gruff voice: "Son, this isn't a
battle, it's a war. And it's constant; it will
never stop."

He continued: "Some days you will
win all the battles and some days you
will lose the battles. But never stop
fighting, my son. Never give up!"

That day my life changed forever! I
looked at things from a different
perspective. I looked at myself as me and
my other self as the addict. After this, I
started to look at myself as a being that
was split into two parts: two 'me's. One
was the addict and the other was the new
me; the person I wanted to be. I knew
when I was drinking and when I was
thinking about drinking it was stinking
thinking, and I knew that was not the
person I wanted to be.

This meant that when I acted on my temptations, whatever they may have been, the addict was holding more shares than I was. And this was preventing me from being the person I yearned to be.

I knew that when I thought like this, or gave into any kind of temptation, the addict side of me took more shares, and that the more shares the addict took the less of the me I wanted to be was left.

When the addict held more shares, he also had more control over me. Just like in business, there would be a company takeover, and in this case the company in question was my mind, my body and my soul.

So with this in mind, every time temptation came along I would refuse to give in and I would win more shares back. I was retaking the company. The more I resisted, the more shares I gained, until eventually I was the major shareholder.

When I own the most shares, I am happy and active, and I achieve more than even I can believe, but when I give into temptation either with my mind, my body or my soul, those shares are again passed over to the other me.

What the old stalwart chap had installed in me was a battle plan: a way of keeping on top of the addiction; a way of keeping the real me in charge of the company.

I am mindful that sometimes the other me who, incidentally, is a sneaky fucker that lies in wait, still exists in the dark reassess of my mind. The other me waits, wanting me to slip up and wanting me to hand over my shares.

I do make mistakes. I'm not perfect, but while I know the other me sits in the darkness waiting, I am in a constant war, fighting battles on a daily basis to hold on to the shares I own.

Remember: Hold on to your shares. Hold the 99% stake in yourself, but never forget that the other you will always hold that 1% and will always pursue the other 99%.

Your Thoughts

HALT!

We have many moods and they change often. With them come many emotions: happiness, sadness, frustration, joy, excitement, despair and fear, to name just a few.

All of these emotions have precursors; things that shape our moods. For the most part we believe them to be external. We allow ourselves to be affected by the actions of others, whether in the written word or by what people say to us directly or behind our backs.

To combat this, we have to build and armour. As Batfink would have said, we establish a "shield of steel".

But how? What's the cause?

We allow ourselves to be easily affected by many untruths. We let others influence our moods far too much. The gossip-mongers, the naysayers and the 'negheads'; we let them in far too easily.

I have found through my limited experiences that a lot of the time the true reason we let people affect us and our moods is that our armour is insufficient.

Four of the main mood affecters are not actually external. Like most things that trouble us, they are internal. These four precursors to mood changes are reasonably simple things to combat. Let's look at the name of this section and decipher what it means.

H = Hungry. When we are hungry, we tend to become low in spirit and easily annoyed. The smallest things, the ones that normally wouldn't affect us, seem to multiply and feel ten times worse than they actually are. When we are undernourished we can feel weak. Headaches and pains that are trivial seem to hurt more and more. All in all, being hungry affects our emotions and tends to lead us to anger.

A = Angry. Being angry can be very dangerous; it can seriously fuck us up! When we are angry we tend to make rash decisions that we often regret. Decisions made through anger are very rarely thought through and more often than not the consequences are more detrimental to us than to those it is directed at.

L = Lonely. Loneliness is a silent killer. It slowly seeps into us, and when it infects us it seems to grow at a phenomenal rate. Loneliness leads to low self-esteem, as we often start to believe that no one cares for us; that no one wants us. Low self-esteem then takes root and grows until we feel depressed to the point of weakness. Then the tears flow and tiredness comes knocking.

T = Tiredness. Tiredness is one of the worst feelings we can harbour. When we are tired, the smallest molehills we have to climb as part of our daily routines take the shape of mountainous peaks. The slightest problem becomes a huge crisis and often makes us feel as though we want the day to end as soon as possible. It actually has us wishing our lives away!

Each one of these precursors is a massive trigger for bad moods, depressive moods, angry moods and frustrated moods. Together, they are the harbingers of depression and destitution. We need be mindful of them at all times and pre-empt their arrival.

So here's the positive bit.

Starting to feel **Hungry**? Don't wait to eat. Eat! Carry a small snack with you. Think about the day ahead and plan for when you will feel hungry. Make the necessary arrangements so that you stay fed all day long.

Keep **Anger** at bay. When we have full stomachs, the world always seems a better place. Even the most annoying people are easier to handle when we have a satisfied appetite. Staying well fed tends to keep anger at bay for me.

Defeat **Loneliness**. Get out there, make arrangements, get together with friends, and join clubs and societies. if you can't get a babysitter, get your friends to bring their children with them. Share the load: your house one week, their house the next, and make a night of it together. Stay in touch with your family, meet the neighbours, set up games nights and pool the childminding duties with trusted family members. Whatever you do, don't let loneliness seep in and take root.

Stave off the **Tiredness**. Get plenty of rest. I know it's hard when life passes us by so quickly. There are so many single mums and dads that just can't find the time as their days are full to brimming.

I have experienced it and I know that it's hard work. For example, the working couples who have to take the kids to school and then go to work and be back again for the bath time. By the time you finish you don't even have time to unwind and relax. I know it's hard, but you must try and make time for rest times. Again, try to do a sleep swap in the day with your friends: a good hour's power nap while one has the kids, and then swap over. Make your sleep a good, wholesome, deep sleep. Prepare your room for sleeping; do not make it an extra lounge. In fact, ban the TV, the laptop and the phone from the bedroom. You will definitely sleep better.

Remember: HALT. Hungry, Angry, Lonely and Tired: negative mood changers. Be mindful of them and pre-empt them, or they will tear your shields down and rip your armour off.

Your Thoughts

Where is the Love?

The world is complex; people are complex. We are surrounded by oxymoronic people, places and statements that confuse and beguile our minds like the ever-perplexing conjurer of magic seeking to misdirect our thoughts while pulling the proverbial wool over our eyes.

Everywhere we look we are bombarded with strategically enhanced marketing, engineered by ivory-towered money men who only seek to separate us from the investment of energy we have made during the last five days of our labour.

Around the world, sycophantic religious zealots who hide behind self-seeking walls of shame are purging their so-called people because they themselves have lost all faith. The dirty nickel and the fast dollar have now taken the place of their once-revered higher power.

Corporate whores seek to enslave
the youth of today inside a racketeered
world of cattle-prodded,
zombielike habitués that stalk the aisles
of the nearest misconstrued palace of
wonderment, offering the latest and
greatest technologically advanced, soul-
satisfying gizmos and gadgets that totally
lack beneficence.

We live in a world of power-hungry
presidents who seek to line their own
pockets while building machines of mass
destruction and billion-dollar floating
marvels that bring about instantaneous
death, while the children of hopeful
voters go hungry and lack education.

Greedy bankers and bailouts are
strewn across the nation's morning
papers and the constructors of society's
downfall sit scoffing at them over
morning tea at The Ritz.

Boys are marched off to fight bloody
wars around the world under false
promises of career and job satisfaction,

while the recruiters sit back and take tea with the so-called enemy.

The world is dying as a result of the gratuitous invention of man's so-called improvement of life, and we stand by and watch as a once-wonderful world is raped of the resources that are consumed by many but benefit few.

People are bullied into early deaths by people they have never met for reasons we will never know in thousand-mile-apart conversations held at midnight. Loneliness and low self-esteem are spread via the world wide web of deceit, which hides its ugly head behind promises of love.

I ask you people… **WHERE IS THE LOVE?**

"Spread love everywhere you go, let no one ever come to you without leaving happier."

Mother Teresa

Your Thoughts

Decisions, Decisions

We all face decisions on a daily – no wait, make that an hourly…no, erm, a minutely, or hold on, I mean secondly basis – I think. You know, sometimes I just can't make up my mind.

Decisions are sometimes very easy to make, especially if we can see that they benefit us. But sometimes a quick decision can turn into a nightmare scenario.

Take the shopping channels on TV, for instance. These channels are designed for people who make quick, poorly thought through decisions. They are designed to take your cash before you've even thought about what you are buying. They do this by showing you all the benefits of a product without pointing out any of the pitfalls.

"Buy it now," they say, "only ten left in stock." Or: "Quick! Get it before it's gone." Have you ever noticed that the people selling those products always seem to have one themselves? Yeah, right. Where do they live? In a warehouse?

Like most salespeople, these salespeople don't even sell you the product; they sell you the dream based around the product. It's never just a necklace or a ring, it's a "romantic gesture given to a loved one who deserves it" (because we've just told you so). I have never seen a salesperson just sell the product. They always sell the dream.

It's all around us: people selling dreams, day in, day out, and people making quick, poorly thought through decisions.

I was recently talking to a group of friends about the traditional UK holiday parks that sell us the dream. How wonderful they make it look; all glossy, clean and populated by the nicest people you could ever meet.

I went on one of these holidays. I handed over my hard-earned cash for the dream they promised me: fine dining in quiet restaurants filled with smiling families, fun nights out with entertainment to warm the heart, and state-of-the-art swimming pools with changing facilities in which you could eat your dinner off the floor.

Instead of the dream I had paid for, I was presented with a room that I wouldn't put a gentleman of the street in, a dining hall that resembled a St Trinian's school hall fight and a nightclub full of drunken adults and lost children. We were all after the same colourful dream we had been mis-sold on the TV and in the brochures, but instead we were offered a swimming pool filled with floating turds the size of King Kong's fingers.

The holiday had been a quick decision, because in those days money burnt holes in my pocket and rather than blowing it all on get-rich-quick schemes I wanted to treat my young family. My life has been full of quick decisions until now, and look where they got me. Not that far, I can tell you.

All the good decisions in my life have taken time. I've thought them through and have looked at the benefits. But somewhat more importantly, I have looked at the pitfalls. I take my time these days over big decisions and that way I don't get burnt too easily and I don't repeat the mistakes of the past.

I find that good people are willing to wait for you to make a decision if it's the right one; if it's beneficial for both parties involved. I find that the salespeople who really trust what they are selling give you time to make decisions. They give you all the information you require, good and bad. I find that those who truly want you to achieve, who truly want you to succeed, those who are sincere about you, will give you the time you need to make the right decision.

A good decision is thoroughly thought through and the consequences are weighed and measured. Ask yourself: do I need it? What's the cost (in monetary, emotional, mental and physical terms)? Is it a fair and ethical two-way transaction?

Remember: Some decisions have to be made quickly, but if you can take your time and think them through, do so. That way you will end up happy with the decisions you make... I know I am.

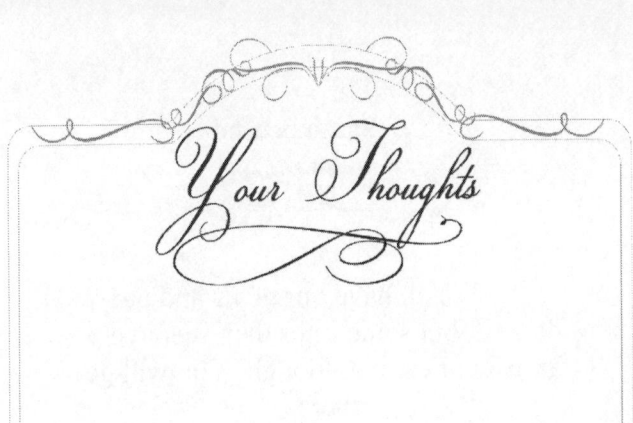

Your Thoughts

Stay Focused

We all have our goals and our dreams, but sometimes they seem very far away. Fear not, though. You will get there.

We have to stay focused on our goals and our dreams. Life has a way of testing us to see if we are really ready to have what we crave. Life will throw up obstacles and tests. It's life's way of asking us: "Are you sure this is what you want?"

Sometimes we are forced to take a road that seems a million miles from what we aspire to be or have in our lives. If we have faith and stay focused on our goals we will reach them without a doubt, even if it seems as though we are running in the wrong direction at times.

Life will sometimes push us in a direction that confuses us and makes us think we are on the wrong track, but I know based on my experiences that this is life's way of giving us further knowledge so that we can achieve our dreams.

If we fail a test it's because we were not ready. It doesn't mean we can never pass that test; we just need more knowledge to enable us to do so. Sometimes that knowledge has to come from a source we are not used to gaining knowledge from, but if we stay focused that source will teach us what we really need to know.

Many times I have been on a journey towards a goal when I have been diverted onto a different path, but that path has always taught me something about my long-term goal.

Knowledge comes in many shapes and sizes, and from many different sources, but I believe all the lessons we have – whether they are expected or not – teach us what we need to know to achieve our dreams, even if we aren't convinced of it at the time.

So expect the unexpected and when it comes, ask yourself: what can I learn from where I am now, and how will it help me achieve my goals and dreams?

Remember: Stay focused on the end goal. Do not give up trying to achieve it and it will surely happen. There is always light at the end of the tunnel.

Your Thoughts

The Challenge

Trying to achieve our dreams isn't easy. It's really hard, in fact, but the good news is, it's meant to be. The challenges and obstacles that get in our way are there for a reason, so don't run away from. Embrace them.

On every little step of the journey towards your dreams you will be challenged and asked to step up to the mark. You can do one of two things: you can either step up or you can step down. But when you step down, the likelihood is that you're going to get run down, too.

Every personal challenge in life has two outcomes: victory or loss. There is no in-between, there is no draw. A draw just means that you didn't win. You may not have lost, but you still didn't win. Sometimes, drawing is worse than losing, especially when you're drawing against yourself.

Winning is the key!

Life's challenges come when we need to be taught a lesson, and the harder they are the more we need the lesson. Life brings these lessons to our feet because we cannot move forwards unless we take on the challenge and win.

It's no use sitting on your backside and waiting for the challenge to go away, because it won't! It will not go away until you get up and face whatever it is head on. You cannot move past the challenge to your goal until you face it and beat it.

It could be something as simple as getting up an hour earlier to achieve something you need to achieve, or it could be facing your worst fear, but either way the challenge will still be there every second of every day until you take up the gauntlet and face it head on.

The good news is, the challenge is never as big as we make it out to be. Often these challenges seem massive in the mind, but often when we actually face them and take action we can't understand what all the fuss was about. It's never as bad as we think it's going to be.

So, when a new challenge presents itself at your feet, stand up and face it head on. There is a lesson to learn in every challenge, and lessons lead to knowledge. The more knowledge we gather on the way to achieving our goals and dreams, the more use we will get out of them when we get there.

It will be hard, and if it isn't it's not really a challenge anyway. It will use up your energy and it may even be physically challenging, but if facing that challenge head on propels you even one inch closer to your dream, pick up the gauntlet and slap the face of your next challenge with it. I promise you will not regret it.

144

Remember: A challenge is there for a reason. We are challenged because we need the lesson that lies within that challenge. We need it if we are to achieve our dreams.

Your Thoughts

A Different Perspective

Millions of years have passed since the attack started. They are everywhere. Our world is in chaos. They came up from the ground and invaded; stripping the planet of all its resources, killing anything that got in their way. Destruction is everywhere. The young barely have time to grow before they are used as sustenance and the old are destroyed without thought. Those who are in between fall from the constant onslaught.

We once lived without chaos – we lived in harmony – but since they arrived, nothing has been sacred. Nobody is untouched. Life once flourished, but now death is everywhere. We struggle to survive, when previously our only aim was to provide. Such is the extent of the devastation that some of our species are now extinct.

The loss of our kind is now entering a critical phase. We no longer roam free as we once did. We are fighting a chemical and concrete war; a war that we fear we cannot win. We are victims of the non-stop decimation of our planet. Fear of extinction is everywhere.

We are periodically taken away and chemically changed beyond our normal functionality. We have become experiments for the invaders that only benefit their kind. We are so weak now and our planet is dying.

The invaders see that we are all connected and that they are dependent on our survival for theirs, but they continue to invade and wipe out our kind day after day. When we are gone they too will perish. They will share the same fate as us: a slow, agonising, suffocating death.

If only we could communicate with the invaders. If only we could show them that the progressive extinction of our people and our world will in fact herald the signing of their own death warrants.

Deep down they know, but they do it anyway.

We are hardy and we will continue to rise up where possible. We will never give up the fight to redress the balance. If only they could understand us before it is too late. There could be hope, but alas, hope is all we have.

Why don't these invaders realise the importance of balance?

We are nature. We are the green grass, the fields, the vegetation and the trees. We plead with our human invaders to listen, but as yet they have not. We fear that the end has already been created, but we live in hope.

Sometimes we can't see the problem because we are looking at it from the wrong perspective. We have to reposition ourselves so that we can see the problem from another perspective. This prevents us from being so short-sighted and allows us to think more about how we can help others, and in what ways.

Remember: We don't all see with the same eyes or think with the same mind.

Your Thoughts

The Snowball Effect

Used in a positive way, the snowball effect is the tipping point of success, but what does it really mean and how do we make the snowball effect happen?

The snowball effect occurs when you get to a point where the work is done; the point at which it not only speaks for itself, but is so successful that it sells itself.

The first thing we have to understand is that there can be no snowball effect without first having a snowball. The snowball is the starting point for the snowball effect. In this case, the snowball is your current project; the one you're working on right now, or should be!

If we take a literal look at the making of a real snowball and how it is created, we can compare it with the ways we can achieve our current projects or, ultimately, our long-term goals. First we have to gather everything that is needed to create our snowball in this case (snow, in this case). We have to gather each flake and every frozen drop of water we need and mould them into a shape that will roll.

We have to be mindful that if the snowball is packed too loosely it will fall apart, while if we pack the snowball too tightly it will become misshapen rather than the smooth, spherical shape that is needed for it to roll and attract yet more snow, which allows it to grow. To get the snowball right it has to be shaped using just the right kind of snow and just the right amount of pressure.

Once the snowball is created, we have to take it to a great height from which it can be pushed. It requires enough pace to grow into a powerful force that can break down barriers, smash through walls and ultimately become an avalanche of raw, unstoppable force. It is only when we take it to the top of the mountain and drop it off that we find out whether or not the snowball will roll or be smashed into a thousand pieces.

If we use this example of a real, physical snowball as a blueprint for reaching our goals, we cannot go far wrong. We need to understand that, like the snowball, our projects first have to be built in such a way that they become the avalanches we desire.

In order to create these avalanches, we first have to gather everything that is needed to achieve our ultimate goals: self-selling projects of immense power. By using the word self-selling, I am not just talking about project or products that have monetary value, although this blueprint also works for that.

This blueprint can be used for work, for that 'perfect' relationship, for a change of direction or for that elusive long-term goal we keep falling short of scoring. If we want to break down barriers, smash through walls and sit in the company of the people we consider inspirational, we will need to work hard, make sacrifices and risk pain and failure. I have learnt more from my failures than I ever have from my successes.

To create that avalanche of self-selling power, we have to first understand that we will create misshapen work; work that has been overworked or underworked; work that carries too much or too little pressure. Before we can create a shape that will, grow like the snowball, we will have to know pressure, pain and failure. But once we get it right, the avalanche will surely follow.

Our work must be moulded, tested through pressure and finally shaped into something so substantial that it will stay in shape long enough to withstand its fall from a great height (the scrutiny of our peers and potential customers, for example).

It is only then that we will be able to take it to the top of the proverbial mountain and throw it over the side, into the abyss. It is only after we throw it off the mountain (put it in the public domain) that we find out whether the work, effort and time we have invested is enough, because if it's not it will be smashed apart.

If it is smashed into a thousand pieces, we can do one of two things: we can accept failure and give up on our dreams of achieving the snowball effect, or we can stay on the mountain, gather more of what we need and start again, knowing that we either put in too much of the wrong effort or not enough of the right effort. Then we can adjust accordingly, ready for our next attempt. If we get it right, we can enjoy the snowballs' gathering effects and all they attract as they grow into avalanches of achievement.

Remember: It is only after many failures, many seconds, hours, days, weeks, months and even years of gathering the things we need, testing them out under pressure and failing many times that our proverbial snowballs will be substantial enough to carry the weight, power and pace they need to sit alongside those that have already managed to create the all-gathering snowball effect.

Your Thoughts

It's Only a Test

"How many times do I have to be tested?" I often cry. "How many times do I have to be put through the burning flames of the forge? How many mistakes do I have to make? How many times do I have to fall down the slope and how many times do I have to slip back down the rungs of the ladder before I get it right?!"

Then I sit in silence and listen, for it is then that the answer comes. And it's not the answer I want to hear it; it is the answer I need to hear. "As many times as it takes!"

Life is refining me because I want to better myself. I want to achieve something – to add purpose to my journey through life – and for this to happen I have to be refined. It's no good trying to live a better life while making the same old mistakes and dead-end decisions. For my life to have purpose, for me to grow and move forwards, I have to be refined.

The old chunks of want, self-destruction, violence and greed have to be slowly filtered away in order to let the new me shine through. The trouble is that I, like many of us, want the process to be quicker. I want it and I want it now!

There is nothing wrong in wanting a better, more prosperous life, but we have to understand that change comes at a cost, and that cost is the process of being refined. It's no good trying to move forward and to fit into the narrow spaces where success lies when chunks of our past lives are still sticking out, blocking our pathways to success.

The refining stage is hard, and it's meant to be. It's what takes away all our burrs and ridges of old and allows us to slip through into the narrow gaps of success. These gaps are very small and they have very smooth sides, so if any aspects of our old selves are sticking out we will be unable to smoothly fill the gaps and achieve the success we desire.

We are like finely made swords that have to be put into the forge again and again in order to make the metal stronger and more durable. The stronger the steel, the sharper the blade.

We have to understand the refining process. We have to welcome it in and embrace it. We have to learn from it, because it points out our flaws, enabling us to work on them and smooth them out. It's not a short process, it's a long process, and it's meant to be. It is meant to filter out the weak; to separate those that don't really want success from those that do.

Remember: If, like me, you're in the refining process, stick with it. Look for the ridges, the burrs and the sharp edges and start smoothing them out, because the opportunities for success are plentiful but the gaps are narrow.

Your Thoughts

Fresh Eyes

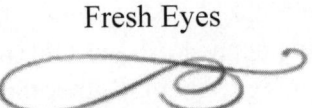

Many times in our lives we become so embroiled in what we think life is, we can no longer see it for what it really is. It may be our jobs, our businesses, our relationships or even a hobby or sport we once loved that now seems to have gone stale. The things we once loved have lost their shine because we have become so used to doing them. They have become monotonous.

That job we craved the night before the first interview has become mundane, that trip to the gym or the five-a-side match we used to take part in for fun has become more like a chore than an activity we used to look forward to. The partners we brooded over and at one time would have walked over broken glass for to get just one kiss become the people we merely share the sofa with, watching TV shows filled with empty, unfulfilled characters that reflect the way we feel.

We even shush our children instead of listening to them. Rather than cuddling up and sharing our hearts' desires with the ones we love, we bury our heads in the world of Facebook or some other social networking site, looking at the exciting lives other people are leading compared with the long, boring days and nights we spend wishing we were somewhere else or someone else.

Sometimes we get so embroiled in this day-to-day pile of lies and bullsh*t that we start to believe this is all that is on offer. As a result of our own actions, our lives have become so routine that our worlds shrink. The walk to our once-exciting jobs makes us feel as though we are trudging down the green mile on the way to the electric chair with the sound of "dead man walking" ringing out in our ears.

That game of darts or pool with our friends has become so competitive that it causes more pain than pleasure, and nights out with our loved ones are so rare that when the opportunity does come along we find they would rather go out with their mates because they've spent the last three months cooped up with you on the now-sagging sofa we once loved seven days a week. Like our relationships, keeping the sofa tidy has become tedious and it's easier just to leave it.

Yes, once the routine sets in and the boredom takes hold, life starts to fall apart and relationships form bigger cracks than the Grand Canyon. In fact, they are so big, with sides so far apart that we can't even see we have fallen into them. We start to seek new pleasures to fulfil the once-satisfying feelings of old.

Ugly thoughts based on unsatisfied desires creep into our heads, populating our minds with blame and envy. The once-beautiful work colleague has become the tart at work and cries of "I don't know who she thinks she is" run through our minds. In some cases these thoughts roll off our tongues. Instead of taking responsibility for our own thoughts, we try to blame everyone else, and this results in us slagging them off.

The petite princess whose cute little giggles once made us drunk with love has become the harsh cackle of the witch whose bum does actually look big in that dress.
The prince who once rode a white stallion and swept you off your feet has turned into a donkey riding drunk with a roaming eye for the village wench, normally the tart at work or the one-time best friend who always seems to be living a better life than us. Yes, the more we let monotony, routine and boredom take hold, the worse our thoughts and our lives become.

We don't mean for this to happen, nobody ever does. It just seems to happen. We slowly forget the reasons why we did the things we did or do, and why we formed the relationships we are in. When life becomes a daily, stomach-churning routine of the same old, same old, we need to take stock. We need to stop and take a look at our lives. We need to think about OUR lives; the ones WE created, and ask ourselves (which most of us probably have if we are honest), where did it all go wrong?

One of the greatest things I ever did was to create two lists. In AA, they call this an inventory. One included all the things in my life I hated and one included all the things that I loved. The former was rather longer than the latter, I can tell you. The two lists allowed me to see in black and white, in plain sight, what exactly had made my life so miserable. The answer nearly always comes down to choices. I know we can't control some of the things that happen in life, but we can control how we react to them. We just have to practise more.

If you try writing these two lists, you'll probably think before you start that they won't be that long, but once you start writing you will find it hard to stop. These lists make us realise just how much we think we like about our lives compared with how much we really do like.

After I first wrote my two lists more than twelve years ago, I made a plan to make the 'likes list' bigger than the 'dislikes list'. To do this I had to change the way I lived. I did this on a weekly basis, chipping away at the dislikes and building on the likes.

It worked. I found that to build the likes I had to try new things, meet new people, find new challenges and face up to my fears. And the dislikes? I just had to stop doing them. I hated being uneducated, so I went to college and got a diploma. And I liked it. So I studied more and gained an HND. I carried on with education and I was meeting new people along the way. I was doing new things, discovering new talents and creating positive events in my daily life. In fact, my education went so well that I ended up with a Bachelor of Science degree.

I know! Even I was shocked when I found out.

When I did the lists and worked on them, I found that I was doing so many things I liked that I never really had time for the things I disliked. I found that when I created my lists and worked on changing them, I looked at my life differently. I saw the things I needed to change and I changed them. The lists changed and my life changed too.

Remember: If your life has become monotonous and the cracks are starting to appear, write the two lists. It will help you look at your life with fresh eyes. I'm off to update mine right now.

Your Thoughts

Conclusion

As you have read, I have found a way of expressing my feelings; not like in the days of old, in a negative way, but in a positive way. In a way that I hope will help others.

My writing is a way for me to dump my dark thoughts. I write the dark thoughts down every day and press delete, clearing the way for the good thoughts to come through. I can no longer sit in deep depression and let the dreary, dark thoughts take over my daily life. I have no time for them; I have a life to live.

So now when I write it isn't the dark feelings that make their way to the forefront of my mind, it's the bright ones; the ones full of love that allow me to live in a happier place.

The days of going to bed full of fear are gone and the mornings of waking up dreading the day ahead have dissipated. Instead, I look forward to the day ahead when I wake up. I look at every day as though it is a new adventure. I'm excited about what the new day will bring, the people I will meet and the opportunities that will present themselves.

Because I clear my dark thoughts on a daily basis, I have found that opportunity raises its head more and more these days, and the more clarity of mind I have the more opportunities I see.

I no longer let opportunity pass me by. I no longer sit and wait for that golden ticket to success. I get up, get out there and put myself in the middle of the road of opportunity; so much so that opportunity can't miss me these days. I never, ever, let it pass me by.

Some opportunities are right for me and some are not, but the important thing is that now I see them (in fact, I'm nearly overrun by them on a daily basis), all I have to do is stick my hand out and grab them. I have even found that they slow down for me. They want me to catch them.

Opportunity also wants you to catch it, so get out there in the middle of the road. Don't dwell on things, don't wonder about what might have been, don't let opportunities pass you by. Take a chance, run towards your dreams, be kind to yourself, work hard and always remember…

LIFE IS GOOD.

Peter Skillen: author, writer, filmmaker, teacher and twelve-step warrior.

14200824R00108

Printed in Great Britain
by Amazon.co.uk, Ltd.,
Marston Gate.